CONTEMPLATION

PAULIST PRESS / New York   Paramus   Toronto
in cooperation with
NATIONAL CATHOLIC REPORTER
P.O. Box 281, Kansas City, Mo.

JAMES CARROLL

CONTEMPLATION

Liberating the Ghost of the Church
Churching the Ghost of Liberation

24813

Contents

Speaking for Myself   9

1 Ghosts of God   14

2 Mortification for Liberation   36

3 The Right to Ritual   58

4 The Counter Culture Contemplates   76

5

*The original pen and ink drawings
throughout this book
are by
Greg Wilhelmi*

For my friend
Al Moser

Speaking for Myself

YOU may remember the story. It was widely
reported in the summer of 1971. The vio-
lence in Northern Ireland was in its seventh
blossoming, and the story of the shot priest
caught the tragedy of a whole people, a whole
age.

A young Belfast workingman, Catholic, was
returning home of an afternoon when he was cut
down by British guns in one of those increasingly
common and seemingly "unintended" incidents
of death. A young priest from a nearby church

ran with his oils and purple stole to the man where he lay in the street. While the priest mumbled the last rites over the fallen workman, a second shot rang out from England. The priest slumped in sacred gesture, falling himself over the man he was anointing, dead. One thinks of Jesus, who responded to death by dying.

Those of us who are believers still, believing for our own sakes and not for our parents' or our children's, are discovering that the easy gestures of belief are losing their exemptions from real life. The collapse of the Catholic Culture, and of our certain dogmas of Church and Nation, reveals us to ourselves. We are exposed. We can no longer hide behind sacraments or rituals or forms or formulations. The holy water font, like the levee, is dry.

The Irish priest left the rectory. He left the ritual, or it was taken from him. He dropped the oils. The stain of blood made its own stole on the purple ribbon he wore around his neck. A death band. His last Last Rites. The world conspired with war and a passing workman to make the Belfast priest respond to death by dying.

One thinks of Jesus. One falls silent. We are not Irish or bleeding. We have not been flushed out *that* way yet. But still, here we are in the middle of the street, waiting for the final noise. Mumbling to ourselves and to each other.

The essays in this book were written in that street. These are words that arose from my si-

lence when the voices of the gods began to argue
with each other. We are caught in the crossfire
of our warring idols. We must speak, we have
discovered, for ourselves. As we must believe,
not for someone else, but for ourselves. It is time
to stop hiding. The world conspires with wars
and no peace to flush us out. We can blame our
belief on no god. Nor can we continue to en-
slave ourselves in the name of the nearest handy
parent or child. All our idols have fallen and
all our gods have fallen silent. We must speak
for ourselves.

I speak for myself here. The essays in this
book are not something I did for you, or for the
"people" or for the "Church." I wrote them for
myself, a bit of warm breath (hot air?) over the
chaos waters. I was trying to tell the truth.

I am glad to share them with you (people,
Church). I am glad to give away what was given
to me. Of course, these essays are the result of
an infinity of influences, some very particular,
very fleshy. Rick Casey, an editor of National
Catholic Reporter, was helpful and kind while
I was preparing these pieces. Thanks, Rick.

John Kirvan, my present editor, is the cher-
ished villain who taught me to prize writing
more than football when he was my teacher
years ago. Though people who love football are
better off, he is my good friend and teacher still.
Thanks, John.

Michael Hunt is my most avid reader; he likes

my writing because I steal the best of it from
him. He is my colleague at Boston University,
my companion through haunted evenings that
have made us friends. Thank you, Michael.

Greg Wilhelmi, whom I have never met ex-
cept in his art, walks gingerly on the underside
of my words. I am glad to be understood. Until
we meet in the usual way, thanks, Greg.

We have come to understand that the people
who are important to us are the ones with whom
we find ourselves exposed, vulnerable, street-
ridden. Perhaps, we are always thinking, we
should have stayed in the rectory. We are not
Samaritans, after all. We leave our dark corners
and lace curtains not to heal someone, however.
Not even to anoint. Not to bend over some poor
fallen fellow. We are here because *we* are the
ones whose worlds are blown away like powder.
We need no cool Samaritan care. We are heal-
ers to each other, as we are each other's victims. We share, we bear bullets from the same
gun.

The Belfast priest responded to death by dying. He anointed the fallen with his blood, and
was so anointed in return. The new sacrament
we discover is the world's old one: blood brother-
hood, sisterhood. One thinks of the priest in
Belfast. One thinks of Jesus. One falls silent.

S OMETHING new and remarkable is happening. Something old and commonplace. It is happening to me and, likely, it is happening to you. It is happening to many men and women who still struggle to make sense of their clinging belief in Jesus Christ and his Church. A kind of humble and quiet daybreak is coming.

In this decade of failed reform we have been disappointed too often to expect or demand another miracle of God, much less of the Church, but still a fresh and positive mood, a contagion of modest hope, is spreading among faithful men and women who have, in repeated disillusionment, discovered a new depth to their belief. I am one of them. I am working now with these words, trying to name the modest hope, to give flesh to the mood we share.

I believe that we are discovering again these old facts; the only reason to be the Church is to be religious; the only reason to be religious is to pray; the only reason to pray is to love God; the only reason to love God is to love the world; the only reason to love the world is to love each other. What I would like to do in these pages is describe our common rediscovery of the contemplative spirit that is making us religious people again.

The Church Is Dead: Long Live the Church!

It is an idea of Buddhist mystical psychology that the deepest enlightenment, the richest discovery of self and of the other is preceded by some great crisis or acute loss, by something which so shakes the personality at its deepest-down roots that the soul is sent spiraling down to its center point where, finally, God is met. (See William Johnston's excellent book, *The Still Point*.) Something like that has happened to us. The shock of ten years ago when we began to understand that the changeless Church was about to change was nothing compared to the more recent shock which has come as we have understood that the "eternal" Church as we think of it is already in the throes of death.

Though the entire Christian Church is together in this, the Catholic attitude toward its own episcopal leadership is a particularly telling sign of Church demise. No one expected the fall synod of Bishops to do anything significant. The leaders of world Catholicism, as the world nearly

breaks with pain, spent their energy and resources, as we expected they would, in keeping
the past and the Pope upon their common
throne. Who was surprised? Who has not learned
yet that the Church is not its leaders? Or its
schools. Or its parish plants. Or its past. Or its
debts. Or its empty seminaries. Death is written
all over those walls, like some graffiti.

As I write this a crew of wreckers, demolition
men, prepare to collapse the remaining charred
walls of our chapel here at Boston University.
An arsonist, unnamed still, set fire to the building last year. The night of that fire much more
than wood and stone burned. I burned. My easy
belief in a whole way of being a Christian
burned. In the light of fire I saw clearly what my
bones had known for some time: the new Church
was not going to be what we thought it would be;
the new liturgy was not going to be the miracle of
community they promised us; the new social
conscience was going to end neither the war nor
the marriage of religion and America's worst
prejudice. The new relevance means, we have
learned, that President Nixon's words of praise
for Billy Graham are written by a Jesuit. The
new morality of love has meant that people could
break their promises to each other and to God
without feeling guilty. The new burst of feeling
has left us without passion. The new spirit of
community has left us, in the end, alone.

We have been shocked to the deep-root. The

place where we first touched the silence, the song and the good news of Jesus has burned. Each of us knows that we can blame no anonymous arsonist. We have done this to ourselves. We reformers have killed the Church's way of being the Church. Though we did it out of love, we would not have been so careless of the past if we had known.

And now? Now we find ourselves wondering if we are, after all this, still in the Church or not. And now, strangely, we find ourselves at prayer. The great discovery waiting in the ruins to be made is this: beyond the collapse of belief there is still trust. God survives the crumbling of the house we build for him. And so do we. Beyond the trivialization of ritual with balloons and bad English there is still worship. Though the face of God shifts we can still meet him in prayer, alone and with others. When I moved through the burnt shell of our chapel the morning after our night of arson, I felt the absence of God so powerfully it became a new kind of presence. Leon Bloy wrote of himself once, "I am especially—never forget it—a worshiper." We *do* forget that we—especially—are worshipers. God lives where we live and we live to celebrate it. The daybreak I detect for the Church is the possibility, by no means certain, that we can return to who we are —praying people who proclaim his presence precisely where God seems to be most absent. The Church can yet become itself, embracing and nurturing its own fundamentals again: worship, the spirit-life, a contemplative vision of man and his world.

The rediscovery by the Church (which is to say by me and, perhaps, you) of its own fundamental identity as a worshipful people is not the same thing as nostalgic recall. Nor is it a flight from social, political responsibility. I am not worried about going back to yesterday's Church. That temptation exists only for those who do not know that yesterday's Church is dead. It may survive in some places as what Toffler calls an "enclave of the past," but I will not be there. We have begun, perhaps without knowing it, a journey without homecomings. The fact that at times we are nostalgic for the Church, for its glory days, reveals to us how thoroughly gone it is for us. The fact that many, including most bishops, cling to the increasingly empty forms and habits of the Church of Once Before causes us some sadness, for the world could well be served by bold and courageous bishops. But they are men like we are. They do not, finally, anger us. I have no need or desire to kill off the Church of Once Before. I am not against it, as I am not a part of it.

We are discovering in the various ruins of God's burned houses a new union with bishops and fundamentalist Protestants and arrogant Ukrainians. We are fellow worshipers of God. That is union beyond law, beyond rite, beyond anger. Though we do not share common visions of man, of Church, of God, of ourselves, we do—still—share a Word with which we talk of all that. We do—still—share a kind of silence. And that is not nothing. I do not excommunicate the past. Neither do I live there.

The rediscovery by the Church of its own fundamental identity as a worshipful people is not a flight from social, political responsibility. On the contrary, once we start praying again and once we take seriously the contemplative vision we are heirs to, we become more socially and politically restless than ever. The American denial of its own best dream is built on the premise that no one sees beneath the surface of things, as no one sees behind the TV screen. If a whole gathering of people begin to see with what Rozak calls "eyes of fire," everything social and everything political is called into question. Far from amounting to a surrender of involvement in social change, the commitment to a religious, worshipful, contemplative way of life is a profoundly political act, with specific implications for everything from prison reform to exploitative trade practices. As Gandhi said, "Anyone who tries to do an act of religion that is not political understands neither religion nor politics." I believe that a worshipful and contemplative way of living, far from denying resistance to illegitimate authority, sustains it beyond mere gestures, through the long and difficult lifetime of building alternate social structures.

One of the curious things about the daybreak I detect in the life of the Church is the fact that it is not coming about through the efforts of any "community," but is a moment of common recognition by lots of different individual people. We have all been thrown back on our own resources. As more and more of our marriages have ended in divorce, as our religious communities have begun to disperse, as our neighborhood organizations have collapsed under the weight of inertia, as our favorite priests and sisters have faded quietly into other worlds, we have all had to discard our glib talk of "community" and our frenzied attempts to make the Church into a T-Group. We are alone.

And the good thing that is happening is the discovery that being alone is not always the same thing as being lonely. The discovery you make when you are thrown back on your own resources is that your own resources are considerable. Solitude, when it is embraced as an essential part of our life's rhythm, is an awesome gift.

All kinds of people find themselves making the dark journey of these days alone. But the darkness is edged with its own kind of light. The aloneness makes possible, for the first time perhaps, real meetings between one's self and others, and God, and one's *very* self. An acceptance and embrace of darkness and solitude is happening now with all kinds of people:

teenagers coming off drugs; older men and women who, having been thrown back on their own when the children left, find themselves surprised by a quiet happiness; young draft resisters in jail or hiding, who discover a garden in the desert of their own self-sacrifice; religious educators who see their students learning nothing and discover thereby that God himself is a kind of nothing after all.

We are all in exile, on the dark journey, with no prospect of homecoming, alone. Yet we live. There is more here than meets the eye. There is more nerve to our nerve than we thought. We have survived not only the passing of our old hopes, but the passing of our new ones as well; the passing of the old Church, but the passing of the new one as well. We have survived not only the breaking turmoil and chaos of the sixties but even this quicksand inertia of the early seventies. We have survived the fallen temple. We have survived the loss of our best friends, of who we thought God was, of our own easy image of ourselves. And we have survived—this is the real wonder—with style and grace. God says to us what one lover said to the other in *Sunday, Bloody Sunday*: "I know I'm not giving you what you want but I'm giving you what there is." And, as Stanley MacNevin says again and again, "It is enough." We who have died are alive. We who walk on the water are wet.

Praying Is Vertical Thinking

When we pray we break bread with what we do not see. We break bread with the dead. We break bread with the future that waits for our making. To pray is to get below the surface of things. Or above it. Praying is "going down" or "lifting up." My instinct about these times of ours is that we are being invited regularly, coaxed even, to step off the surface of things— one way or the other. We are being invited by events, by history, by death and life to nurture what we used to call without embarrassment a contemplative way of living.

But you are not a mystic, right? And neither am I. Mystics are exotic people who wear esoteric clothes, eat abstract food and live in houses lined with ecstasy. Mystics do not exist. Mystics are heroes that people like you and me made up so that we could say real silence and serious praying are someone else's job. Real silence and serious praying are tough. And we are each called to nurture them. More and more lately we know it. We are not mystics, nor are we acid-heads, nor do we live in tree houses. But we are alive. We do see. The fire that torments and consoles burns at the center of our own names. Each of us does his own breathing; that is the beginning of serious prayer. Each of us does his own seeing; that is the beginning of contemplative vision. The next mystic you meet, give him a dime, but don't hide behind him.

Well, how do *we* pray then? If we begin by presuming we are not already praying, we will uncover the old words and methods and use them to feel guilty again. We were always in the outer courtyard looking in. We never kept our resolutions. But we are not monks. Prayer begins with the lives *we* lead, not with the lives of the saints. I presume that, since the Spirit lives in me already, I am already prone to pray. Perhaps the question should be, how do we already pray? How is my seeing already contemplative? What are the rhythms of spirituality that my life already follows? How do silence, solitude, simplicity already touch me? How do I go from where I find myself beginning?

We spend most of our time and energy in a kind of horizontal thinking. We move along the surface of things going from one quick base to another, often with a frenzy that wears us out. We collect data, things, people, ideas, "profound experiences," never penetrating any of them. We sort out impressions, distinguishing, separating, choosing, planning, worrying, wondering. We parade memories, expectations, fantasies, hopes, agonies before our minds which stir like a bored king on his reviewing stand. We are on the move or our minds want to be. The horizon calls us. We have a kind of interior wanderlust that keeps us flitting about the surface of our own lives.

But there are other times. There are times
when we stop. We sit still. We lose ourselves in a
pile of leaves or its memory. We listen and
breezes from a whole other world begin to whis-
per. Then we begin our "going down." Buddhist
mystical psychology suggests that there are nine
layers of consciousness and when the bottom
one, the ninth, is penetrated, a person meets his
true self. I think of an onion, which fairly asks to
be peeled, not because the center is more truly
onion than the surface, but precisely because the
center is as much onion as the surface is. I pay
attention to my deeper-down self not as a denial
of my surfaces—which I love—but because my
surface is itself in my center. Vertical thinking is
a way of paying attention to one's whole self.

And so the rhythm I trust provides me with
times of "going down," as well as times of
"going along." There are times when the parade
of images, words, ideas, dreams, plans and so on
comes to a stop. A kind of silence takes over my
interior life. My breathing becomes as important
and as worthy of my respectful notice as my
thinking, remembering, or willing ordinarily are.
I sit. I kneel. I walk, even, or jog perhaps, as I do
most mornings after dawn. Even my slight run-
ning includes a kind of utter sitting still. A kind
of nothing. Some mornings it is as though I and
my jogging are the same thing. Some evenings I
am not separated from my sitting. Some moments I am not separated from anything. I be-

come the leaves I lose myself in. I am more than
me, more than my friends, more than my times,
more than my small place. I am—it is clear
beyond words at those times—a kind of universe.
I touch a wordless, speechless union when I dare
to sit still in the presence of some gift beyond. I
know I am not mine alone.

At that moment I am close to more than
meets the eye. As a person of faith I have this old
impulse to name the center of being, the flame
within the fire. As a person of faith I have words
to use in this naming which have been given me
by the Church, which is its most precious and
continuing service. The Church offers words
with which to approach the wordless. The
Church offers a language that enables me to dare
stand before the utter silence of my hiddenmost
self. The Church has taught me to say, and enables me still to say before that awesome void,
"God, Father, Abba!" St. John of the Cross says
quite baldly, "The center of the soul is God." I
believe it, though I do not know what it means.
As a person of faith I know that I have no direct
contact with God himself. I meet him in un-
knowing, in chosen belief, which is its own kind
of unbelief, which is like night to the soul.

We are invited, indeed called, to live in that
night, at the edge of our own center, at the edge
of an abyss that is at once where we begin from

and where we end. "One sets out from God," Bloy said, "to go to God." Vertical thinking involves us in a total life's progression. It is more than "praying." It is living with an edge of mystery and a different set of margins about the world. It is not seeing something different but a different way of seeing. Those moments we used to describe as moments of "prayer" are simply times when we practice with special diligence this special eyesight of ours.

We set out from God the benevolent Father and go to God the dark nothing, who is violent in his absence. Yet we love him. Vertical thinking gets below the easy dogmas and the habits of familiarity we have with God and drags us to the edge of deepness we do not understand. There we learn that our trust in God survives the collapse of our dogmas, as the Church survives the collapse of its buildings. My belief in God does not depend on his being gentle with me, or even on his being "there." That discovery teaches me that my respect and even love for my Church and my bishops and my fellow believers does not depend on their being wise or, even, "good." The Church still invites me and enables me to pay attention to my hidden self, my own abyss, where I touch the self of the world and its abyss. The Church gives me words with which to greet the silence and bread with which to feed it.

The Modest Implications
of Contemplative Vision

Contemplation begins and ends in exile. Contemplation nurtures intimate union with all that, on ordinary days, we try to deny. It invites us to face our own exile. We are members of the man of sorrows. Hope does not deny the desert, and the desert is where we, like Jesus, learn to become ourselves. Vertical thinking plunges us to the depths of existence where suffering lives and where the weeping of the innocents goes on forever. That is why we try to hide from our own contemplative instinct, or try to sign it over to our mystic heroes.

Our contemplative vision begins with what our bones know in September and October; we are living here in this place, at this time in exile. I am not at home and neither are you. Unlike the birds I have no nest. I have no place in which to lay down my head. Once I thought with John Kennedy and Martin Luther King and Eugene McCarthy and Bobby Kennedy and before them with Tom Jefferson and Abe Lincoln that I could be at home in America, that I could lay down my head on her dreams of liberty and justice for all. That was before Dallas, Memphis, Chicago, Selma, Los Angeles, Attica. That was before Vietnam. I am in exile in my own country, and so, perhaps, are you.

Once I thought with Pope John and Hans Küng and Teilhard de Chardin and Daniel Berrigan and before them with Isaac Hecker and St. Francis that I could be at home in the Catholic Church, that I could lay my head down on her dreams of spirituality and service to those in need. That was before the great movement of reform begun at the Vatican Council degenerated into bickering over the life styles of priests and nuns. That was before several heroes and more than a few friends quit the Church. That was before I discovered in myself a kind of inert numbness about the faith where once there was passion that risked extremities. I am in exile in my own Church, and so, perhaps, are you.

We are, in very important ways, in exile from each other. You don't have to live in a huge, anonymous dormitory or in a rectory with a crowd of sour priests or in a family of strangers who share grim sweetness to know that, unlike the birds, you have no nest. Who is not, in very important ways, in exile from the times, from the world, from God, from himself even? Contemplation, however it has begun in the past, begins today with that knowledge, because that knowledge alone removes us from our glib and easy surfaces.

When they said to Jesus, "What is it like to be you?", he said, "Unlike the birds I have no nest. I have no place of my own in which to lay down my head." He said, "I am in exile from my country, from my religion, from my family, from you." Our knowledge of Jesus of Nazareth, as of ourselves, begins when we know what it is to be away from home, without a home, with no hope of one.

To be disillusioned is to begin to live. We have it in our power now to be incredibly creative and humble both. We have no choice now but to stand up and begin to live a changed and changing life. And we will be more modest about our expectations now because our proud proclamations have turned out empty too often too recently.

Contemplation is not a new way to be saved, as the Church, even reborn, is not. If the Church and its contemplative, worshipful way of living enable us now and then to rediscover the faint presence of Jesus Christ who alone saves us, it will be worthy of its name. If what belief remains to us helps us be faithful to our "goings along" and our "goings down," it will be enough. If we set for ourselves the political task not of making America and the world pure, but of refusing ourselves to carry its weapons and setting about to dull the weapons others carry, it will be enough. We begin by refusing to accept those many and attractive privileges of wealth and comfort that are won for Americans by America's money wars.

A contemplative vision will not permit us to hide from the blood of children who even now die for want of the food we feed our dogs. A contemplative way of living will not exempt us from the dangerous struggle to make America's best dreams of justice and equality come true. It will engage us beyond comfort.

Contemplation is a way of standing on one's own two feet and staring all idols in the eye—even the idols of the idol smashers, even the idols of oneself. The *only* reason to live is to bear witness to God! The authentic sign of the discovery of God is the discovery of the neighbor, on whose behalf one is willing, finally, to suffer. "To be a man," Chavez says, "is to suffer for others. God help us to be men."

One thing is required of us today. One thing for our politics, for our Church, for our human and non-violent revolution, for our own happiness. What is required of us is sanctity. Holiness. Wholeness. A way of seeing the world that makes the morning's getting out of bed, if not a pleasure, an act of love at least. We are finding new ways to be holy men and women these days. We must share them with each other. We must wait, watch, listen and act in solitude, but also in solidarity. Around the table of death and life, bread and wine, where we can still meet each other, there are sounds to hear if we listen carefully. There is the sound of going down into the abyss and being lifted up, heart and body, not to heaven but to the good earth. There are the sounds of the lively ghosts of God, laughing still with love. There are the sounds of men and women stirring, standing. There is the sound of the season's changing. And wine. There is the sound of day breaking. And bread.

MORTIFICATION FOR LIBERATION

ONE of the things the new freedom of these days means is that we are not allowed to talk about some things anymore. Among those is a subject we used to talk about a lot: mortification. But no more. Mortification is a forbidden subject. Self-denial is sick. Self-sacrifice is masochism. Soldiers who throw themselves on live grenades, monks who whip themselves with leather cords, Catholics who still don't eat meat on Fridays, husbands who don't play around after the sales conference in the big city, priests who don't get married, Irishmen who still quit drinking for Lent—Manichees all. A matter of toilet training gone wrong. Puritanism. The love of suffering. Sick.

Because that sort of criticism of the mortifying impulse was partly true at least, the Catholic people, by and large, have eliminated the word from their vocabulary and the practice from their lives. Like lots of you I have not eaten fish on Friday in years. I have given up nothing but giving up for several Lents. I have denied myself

self-denial. Old scruples tell me now and then I'm being selfish, though I protest I'm really being myself. But I wonder now and then why being myself with all this freedom turns out to be so boring.

The contemplative vision of ourselves, of our world, of God, for which we yearn in new ways comes only when we dare to look at the old word and the old practice of *mortification* again. In these pages I hope to uncover something of the slavery that lives at center points of the new freedom. I hope to touch the liberation, public and personal, that is possible to us when we dare to be mortified, not to death but to life.

Mortification: Act of Radical Doubt

Mortification, the habit of saying "no" to some of one's impulses, can arise from one's fears of simple pleasure, or from what they told us as children: if it hurts, it's holy; if it feels good, suspect it. Mortification, in other words, can be a denial of life. But not necessarily so. It is important for us to rediscover how the practice of mortification can be an essential way of saying "yes" to life and to its truest goods and pleasures.

Mortification at its best arises from a radical doubt. It is the way to raise questions about what everyone takes for granted. Mortification is the way to question the fundamental assumptions of each age and each institution from this standpoint: do they enable or prevent human life to the full? Most consistently, mortification calls into question the perennial human assumption around which men are always dancing—that suffering and pain are to be avoided at all costs. In our times mortification is an activity of radical doubt which questions *these* assumptions; consumption of things, pleasures, and experiences makes a person happy and the more one consumes the better off one is; to sit still is to waste time; the goal of life is to have; whatever (or whoever) is old is obsolete, while whatever (or whoever) is new is good, indeed better; permanent commitment is impossible and undesirable; drugs (from alcohol to acid to aspirin) are good things; sexual liberation means love is the only rule; being radical means denying what went before.

Mortification doubts what is obvious to the blindest eye of our time and place. It arises from a different way of seeing the world. Mortification is the one activity that resists the enchantment of affluence, that raises questions about the bewitching promise of pleasure that the great Western mirage machine turns out in an infinity of packages. Mortification arises from the gut instinct that the Buick is *not* something to believe in. Mortification is the act of knowing that Eastern Airlines lies, that flying away for a weekend is not half so good as walking away an afternoon, that the wings of man are called legs.

Mortification, then, is not the cultivation of private pain. It is not an act of mere piety. Whether it involves old-fashioned practices like "giving up" candy or more faddish experiments with organic food, it is an instinct of discipline and control which accepts limits as positive and creative. And today, in a unique way, mortification implies a political decision against the politics of hedonism and against the economics of consumerism.

The most pressing issue in the world today, political, economic and moral, is the fact that a minority of human beings pursue without limits their own pleasure, while the majority pay for it with their very lives. The affluent minority, which includes us, is hard at it now, trying either to keep the poor majority in bombed submission, or to put them off with a trickle of "developed" pleasures. Even our most "altruistic" and "liberal" impulses to "help" the "masses" are edged by the conviction that everybody wants to be a consumer and a compulsive competitor.

Most of our attempts to sell our systems to the Third World have failed because the "poor" are not so fast as we to turn ends into means. They raise questions about what we "have": why is it better to have fewer babies and more trucks? Especially when the trucks will be obsolete in two years. "The plows of the rich," Illich says,

"can do as much harm as their swords." And
their schools, and their hospitals, and their
roads, and their soft drinks. What is lacking in
our approach to other nations, as to ourselves, is
a mortified sensibility. The goal of mortification,
far from being mere piety, is nothing less than
the transformation of our personal attitudes toward life, nothing less than the transformation of
the public and political reality that takes its
shape from us as human beings.

Mortification is an act of the imagination. It
enables us, by denying our impulses to self-
aggrandisement, to take other people more
seriously, to *imagine* what it is like to be where
they are. Middle class people have tried, either in
religious life or in the radical "movement," to
embrace a kind of poverty, renouncing goods
and money. They have discovered that they cannot in fact become poor in any real way. They
cannot suffer the deepest agonies of deprivation
that go far beyond material goods to a pain of
the spirit that no member of the privileged, educated classes can ever understand fully. Only the
privileged have the privilege of *choosing* to be
poor, which means, ultimately, that they cannot
be poor. Only the poor are poor.

But the mortification of choosing to live without things, possessions or money is worthwhile
because it makes possible an act of imagination
in which someone who is not poor discovers that
his world includes someone who is. Mortifica-

tion is a form of consciousness in which my
world includes yours. By denying myself I can
imagine what it is like for you to be denied.

Mortification is a form of consciousness in
which the awareness dawns that the "oppressed
peoples" are not the only ones who are oppressed. By "denying myself" I discover how
much *I* need to be freed from deadly poverties of
spirit and flesh. As Tony Mullaney says, "I can
be committed to *your* liberation only when I see
how much in need of liberation *I* stand too."
Mortification is the act of imagining that we
stand in need together, even when it seems on the
surface that we do not.

The importance of this dawns on us when we
realize that every problem of personal com-
munication is a failure of imagination, a failure
of one person to see through the eyes of another,
and therefore the failure of one person to see
truly through his own eyes. Beyond the personal
sphere, our entire national state of havoc results
from a continuing failure of imagination as well.
If American war planners were able to *imagine*
what happens when someone drops bombs on
your grandchild's house in the city, they would
never have launched the disastrous bombing of
Vietnam which resulted, as bombing campaigns
had in England and Germany, in the increased
resolution of the bombed people. The American
failure in Vietnam, from its tragic beginnings to
its still remote conclusion, is being written by our

own inability to identify imaginatively and concretely with bombed people and with bombed Asian people in particular.

Contemplation and mortification imply the effort to identify concretely with other men and women. This is the Christian's way of being, as Daniel Berrigan said of his Catonsville action, "concrete about the existence of God." One of the chief problems facing us today is the fact that our culture is set against the act of being concrete. Abstractions and generalizations are all we are allowed. We go to great lengths to avoid what Marcel called the "scandal of the particular." War is wrong, but *this* war is necessary. Individuals are permitted to deal with the generalities, but the concrete, real, day-to-day particulars are handed over to vast bureaucratic organizations in which no one is responsible for anything. *Men* do not wage wars or nurture the spiral of consumerism that impoverishes our spirits and destroys our environments, or treat the imprisoned like animals, or welfare mothers like prostitutes or all of us like numbers. *Men* do none of it. In fact every man deplores it all. The unbelievably complex and deadly bureaucracies *do* it all. We men regret, mildly for the most part.

We have handed our imaginations, together with our consciences, over to huge institutions which dominate our every hope for the future. Do you want a better church? Divide the diocese, have a synod. Do you want better transportation? Build a highway. Do you want better education? Build more classrooms. Do you want a happy marriage? Go to Essalen. Now that we know how to fly planes the size of mountains, it is time to learn to walk again. Now that we know how to prolong life indefinitely with organ transplants, it is time to learn to die again.

Practice for Death

No bureaucracy can do your dying for you (though some can do your killing). You do your own dying. The moment of death is a moment in which each of us must stand on his own two feet and say yes or no. Mortification is what Sebastian Moore calls "practice for death." Mortification believes in death. Mortification knows that death is not a moment at the end. It is going on all the time. Mortification is simply the human choice to live with that knowledge. Mortification refuses to hide from death in any of the modern caves: in affluence, in nation, in religion, in movement. Mortification happens when a person takes responsibility for himself, for his actions, for his living, for his dying. In that moment, and in that moment alone, men take responsibility for each other.

I did not know what mortification was until I met a young black man named Donald. He was a

member of a gang that moved in the neighborhood of the city parish I worked in a few
years ago. Though we spent little time with each
other, we became in some strange way special
people to each other. Though I cringe now to
admit it, he became a kind of project for me. I
"helped" him. He was my own personal poverty
program. He was always in trouble with the po-
lice. He was surly and rude. He was, as it turned
out, addicted to heroin. He was my first "case,"
and he knew enough to hate me for my conde-
scension. When he was finally busted and put in
the horrible city jail, I went to see him. When I
arrived he was in the midst of the agonies of ad-
dictive withdrawal. I had never seen a man suffer
like he was suffering then. I wanted to help him
but there was nothing I could do. There was no
way I could ease his pain. I remember how glad I
was to get out of the jail, both to get away from
his torment and to get outside where I could
smoke. When I touched my lips with a cigarette,
still thinking of Donald, I knew without deciding
that I could not light it. I could do nothing to
gratify his craving for another fix, indeed would
have done nothing. I could not remove his pain.
And since that was so, I neither could nor would
gratify my own minor addiction. It was not a
matter of choice. It was a matter of my body's
rebellion. I quit smoking that day. It was my
only way to be with Donald. It was my only way
to love him. It was my only way to deal with my

own more subtle imprisonments. I did not quit for him. I did it for myself, a meager gesture toward the meaning both of our lives lacked then.

I have resumed smoking and stopped several times since then; I will go through life starting and stopping. But what I learned remains. The only reason to be mortified, to "give up" or to refuse pleasure is to be with another person who suffers, to say with your body, "I can't take it away, I can't even share it really, but I am with you."

Mortification, whether it is going without cigarettes or a large salary, is a symbolic action which proclaims the inner unity of men that contemplative vision sees. The reason it still, even now, is worthwhile to freely go without food occasionally is to say to the hungry who have no freedom about it, "I can't take it away, I can't even share it really, but I am with you." We must seek ways to make the distant sufferings of hunger, of addiction, of napalm, of despairing spirit concrete enough in our own lives to make us know *our* world includes the suffering poor. The world of the suffering poor includes *us,* the suffering rich. Mortification is not a matter of our "helping" or "loving" those who are needy. It is a matter of knowing how each of us is needy. The slave-making forces at work in our world exempt no one. Mortification is an act of resistance against our *own* slavery. It is not a "good deed," but an act of self-interest in its most profound sense.

Mortification is a symbolic action that says something about mankind in *concrete* language. The mortification of a permanent, lifetime commitment to another person in marriage makes concrete the abstract human value of fidelity and the hope men have that God is faithful to his promises. The mortification of celibacy as practiced by men and women of Catholic ministries makes concrete the radical demands that God's presence in the world implies. What has become clear, however, in the recent debates about celibacy for priests is that it points more to the radical demands of a bureaucratic institution than of the Kingdom of God. Celibacy should be restored to its former place as an optional mortification for priests precisely so that its radical character might be realized again.

Ironically I find myself in the position of believing that most of the arguments advanced by people like me in favor of changing the universal discipline of celibacy for priests are inadequate and chauvinist because they spring from our insufficiently mortified sensibilities. To say, as American culture does, that sexual abstinence makes a full life impossible for a man, that every man needs a bed-fellow, is to endorse and continue the idea that the woman exists primarily to satisfy the man's needs, to console him, to support him as he does the world's serious work.

The fact, apparently true, that most priests are lonely and frustrated is a poor reason to change the celibacy discipline; at worst it is a sexist reason. The celibate life is a tough and slightly unnatural way to live. It requires a knowledge of mortification that is as concrete as an empty bed each morning. But it makes sense and its own kind of satisfaction when the needs of the served community and the presence of God and of the priest's own freedom are all more important than his loneliness. We priests could all do with a bit more reality, which is to say laughter, about our own melodrama; *all* life is lonely. The celibacy debate, like the airline ads, does not tell us that.

Another result of the Catholic preoccupation with celibacy is the fact that the spiritual significance of human sexuality has developed mainly in terms of sexual *abstinence.* Unlike the great primitive religions, ours has little sense of making love as an act of profound worship. We apologize to God all the time for the way our flesh "interferes" with prayer. It makes you wonder which religions are *really* primitive.

Most human beings are called to pray sexually. *That* is what matrimony, as a sacrament, attempts to proclaim. Prayer is being concrete about God; the experience of ecstasy is *the* most concrete experience available to human beings, and the most common form of ecstasy is sexual. We were created for ecstasy. Ecstasy is the proclamation that flesh and spirit are one. Ecstasy is the way we tend with our very flesh to the presence in *our* midst of the beyond. Sexual ecstasy involves meeting the beyond in the fleshed partner. The terror, the awe, the (quite literally) trembling, the silence; the sexual moment is overpowering and it is religious.

We have denied the sexual either by shaming it or by idealizing it. What is needed is a spirituality of the sexual relationship which neither shames nor idealizes. Married people are not monks, but the only developed spirituality available to them is monastic in origin and character.

A spirituality for married people begins with the knowledge that sexual love, like celibate love but differently, implies its own kind of mortification. Indeed, the act of intercourse is always and in some way an act of death. It is death with and for the loved partner, and as such is a source of life. Poets from Shakespeare to Eliot often pun on the word "die," using it to refer to both moments.

Both moments of death and sexual love making imply the surrender of control, the giving away of oneself and the call to trust beyond trustworthiness. Death and sex are the moments of high risk, which makes them crucial moments of prayer and self-denial in the other's behalf.

When we talk about sexuality we discover again how hard it is these days to tell your hang-up from your values. That difficulty makes it hard for us to relax with the idea of mortification. Mortification, whether a celibate life or not eating candy, is always in danger of serving our own warped needs to be "pure" or "suffering." I suspect that every act of mortification will have about it a margin of self-grandeur, a bit of martyrdom, a fear of full life, some guilt about pleasure. But there is no human acting that is pure or free of ambivalence. One attitude we can take that will help us to keep in check our tendency to take on suffering for silly, guilt-induced reasons is this: the real limits of our lives offer opportunities enough for mortification. The most difficult, disciplined project for any person is to accept, embrace even, the ordinary limits of his life. Death is already and always at work in us. Mortification is the way we resist it. The promises we make are hard to keep. Mortification is the way we serve them faithfully. Acts of unjust authority, whether of government or church or bureaucracy, threaten continually to deprive us of our freedom and dignity. Mortification is the way we say no to injustice not only as it clutches a distant neighbor, but as it threatens us.

Extraordinary acts of self-denial are often flights from the much more ordinary tasks of day to day living with other men and women. We are not called to be heroes, as we are not called to punish ourselves. We are called to be human beings. There was never a hero yet who wanted to be one. Mortification is a form of humility, for it accepts a small role in the worldwide resistance against death in all its forms. As Howard Zinn says, "We must each resist injustice in our own little places." The hope of the world is that men and women who say "no" to death in the forms in which they confront it are everywhere.

Mortification is the refusal to hide from death; it is the choice to deal with it now. Mortification is the refusal to cooperate in the world's attempt to make victims of us. It begins by rejecting the common and deadly inertia that attacks us at home, in our relations with our loved ones, in our own sense of significance. Mortification is not an act of self-deprecation, as it is not an act of heroism. It is an act of simple, common self-respect. It is what gets us out of bed in the morning. It is the act of daybreak, of rising, of keeping sleep in its place. It is the act of standing up, the act of light in the face of dark, the act of life in the face of death.

Jesus Christ—Mortification of God

The Christian instinct to be tough with death begins with the knowledge that Jesus Christ himself was death made life. Jesus was tough on himself and his followers. He lived what we have no choice to call but a mortified life. He demanded mortification from the men he chose. "If any man would come after me let him deny

himself and take up his cross and follow me."
The paradox to which Jesus points with his life is
that suffering is a prerequisite for happiness.
Discipline is a prerequisite for freedom. Mortification is a prerequisite for liberation. "Whoever loses his life for my sake and for the sake of
the Good News will save it."

It was not mere altruistic love of the other that
led Jesus to suffering; it was love of himself as
well. All men die, suffer, experience utter alienation and hunger to the point of pain. Mortification, "taking up the cross," is rebellion against
all that. It is the refusal to identify with death or
with those who wreak it on the world. Mortification is a form of identification with the suffering
poor, beginning with oneself, but for the sake of
life. The mystery is that at the point of suffering
love God is met. James Douglas says that "suffering is the one earthly reality with which God
identifies himself universally." Since, in the end,
the reason for life is to be with God, the reason
for mortification is the same; in the acceptance,
embrace even, of the darkness, of suffering, of
pain, we meet God. In the absurd moments of
no-meaning God is present to us. The cross reveals all we need to know about God, and that is
a kind of horror. Mortification refuses to hide
from the horror and instead wrestles with it.

The Good News is not only that God is, by his
act of mortification in Jesus Christ, identified
with the "poor" and the "oppressed" and the

"powerless," but that he is identified with us—in *our* poverty, oppression and powerlessness. God teaches us what mortification is by his own commitment to it—an act not of heroism, but of humility, not of self-grandeur but of *kenosis*. Jesus Christ accomplished the ultimate mortification —giving up the pleasure even of his own noble sacrifice. He is the horrible sign to us that religion without crucifixion is meaningless; life without suffering love is a lie; an unmortified Christian life is a sacrilege.

Gandhi said, "Living Christ means a living cross; without it life is a living death." The great apostle of non-violence was at the same time an apostle of mortification. Gandhi knew that the violent, world-destroying habits of men arose from their inability to deal directly, in disciplined fashion, with their death-doing impulses. Think of the celibacy of Gandhi or his fasting or his poverty. Mortification, taken for one's own dignity and that of others, is the decision to suffer in love rather than participate in death-dealing. Mortification is an act of rebellion that begins by resisting one's *own* oppressing instincts and going from there to resist the oppressing instincts of others. Mortification is always and by definition an act of non-violence. The good sense of non-violence and the good sense of mortification are the same. Both believe in the redemptive power of suffering love. Both intend to move oppressors, beginning with oneself, to see all victims, beginning with oneself, as persons worthy of respect. Both believe that crucifixion reveals resurrection, that death opens the way to life.

Non-violence and mortification both spring from the conviction that human life is inexpressibly good and that evil, even in its contemporary forms, is able to be transformed by the human capacity to suffer for love. It is there that God still chooses to live among us. The world calls us to non-violent living. We call ourselves to a kind of dying, the kind that opens for us fulfillment with God forever, beginning with the fullness of life on this earth, on this day, with you, with me, with more than we have words for.

3 **THE RIGHT TO RITUAL**

W E are learning that among the benefits America offers its people are easy entrance to an entire world view, a thorough system of ethical values, and a way of passing both on. In short America offers its people its own kind of religion. The chief advantage of civil religion Americana is that you don't have to be religious to practice it. All one need believe about God is that he is on our side. He lives somewhere between the fourteenth hole, the yacht club, and the foreign aid bill. The good news celebrated is that things will get better, especially for us. The chief value proclaimed is blessed uniformity. More and more, we all look alike and that is the function both of American civil religion and MacDonald's Enterprises Inc. The evangelical impulses of American civil religion are channeled into the national task of building the one holy city; we go forth and Los Angelize all nations in the name of bread that does not come down from heaven. Ecumenism has come to mean the Papalization of Billy Graham, the Nixonization of the Catholic Bishops and the Americanization of God, all celebrated non-denominationally each Sunday in the East Room, where, presumably, the sun starts its rising each day.

The most frightening thing about the death of the Catholic religious culture, symbolized by the collapsing school system and accompanying loss of passion for "Catholic" identity, is the dawning realization that the alternative to the old creaky church is a slick, slightly Gothic version of American civil religion. With what prayer is left to us we pray it is not so.

Rediscovering Time and Space

We are religious not because it is good for our country, but because God exists. Religion is the way we are concrete about his existence. Religion is the way we discover an identity which transcends national groups and factions. Religion offers us standards of judgment and moral choice that go beyond the ultimates of American policy makers. There is more to be considered than "national interest" when it comes to our decisions to export our violent forms of "peace," as there is more to be considered than protocol when it comes to praying at the White House.

What the world needs of us today is a rediscovery of what it means to be religious. The passion must return. Those of us who have been raised in the Catholic tradition are among the people who have opportunities yet to continue and develop the gospel cause of real worship which is real peacemaking. We are judged by the ease with which we identify not with the centers of power but with prisoners.

The rediscovery of religion will begin with the rediscovery of ritual. The chief failure of the liturgical renewal has been the widespread dulling of the once-honed sense of ritual among the Catholic people. I believe that the ease with which even Catholic Bishops move into the bland, esoteric, non-ritualized pomp of East Room services is partially able to be accounted for by the fact that they, like all of us, have forgotten what real worship is like. We have become embarrassed by our pagan roots. Real ritual begins with what people, since primitive times, have experienced as a contemplative sense of time, and a contemplative sense of space. Time and space are when and where men meet God. They are anything but bland or esoteric; they are the when and where of life. The only way to penetrate the times and the places is with the eyes of fire that provoke utter silence and ritual passion when human beings see through them together.

One can understand the problem of our culture as a loss of the sense of time. John Silber, president of Boston University, treated this subject brilliantly in his inaugural address, "The Pollution of Time." He diagnosed our contemporary crisis, saying, "When the structure of time is destroyed, the basis for significance in our own lives is likewise destroyed. All meaning is lost in the instantaneous." I believe that one of the by-products of "instantaneous culture" where everything from coffee to marriage to abortion to ecstasy is available instantly, is "instantaneous religion." We see it in young Jesus freaks who prize the instant of conversion more than the process of search that preceded it and continues after it. We see it in liberated men and women who prize the sincerity of the moment of promise-making more than the difficult and long-haul commitment to be faithful. We see it in Catholic and Jewish leaders who surrender core principles of belief by joining in a state religious observance that is careful to have no past and no future. We see it in new and versatile Church architecture that makes places of worship double as classrooms and gymnasiums; slide this wall, push this button and bingo, it's a church! Bingo, it's bingo!

To perform a religious ritual is to respect the structures of time. Ritual is the act of discovering time, not fleeing it. The discovery that is made when time is taken seriously, ritually, is that time itself opens on, includes, the eternal, the time beyond our times. The religious ritual enables us to step out of time *as we control it* and into that time which is beyond our control.

Ritual is the primordial human way of touching the past and, in mystery, standing in its presence. The chief casualty of our instantaneous culture is the past, the memory of what has gone before. The religious impulse to celebrate the presence, in mystery, of the past runs directly counter to our prevailing cultural instincts, which know little, if any, continuity between past and future. Ritual is the primordial human way of affirming the continuity of past and future, and their presence, in mystery. Ritual celebrates the specific history of the gathered people, and it does so in familiar ways. Gesture, word, posture, clothing, action, calendar, story all combine to remember and to imagine, to memorialize and to anticipate. The presumption of culture is that "this is the way things always were." All of time is focused in the great "NOW." Immense energy is spent eliminating what looks old. The differences of one time from another are denied instead of celebrated.

This is the logic behind what amounts to the cultural mutation that is occurring in our experience of time. The rites of passage, those rituals by which a person marks and facilitates his growth from birth to death, are observed less and less in our period. The rituals of movement through the dark journey and the struggles with the mythic dragon and the progression of signs that mark childhood off from adulthood are growing more and more scarce. Young people strive to look older, as old people strive to look younger. The great human question continues to be, "How do you separate yourself from the past without having to murder it?" Moving from the past into the future in creative and peaceable ways is what ritual enables human beings to do. Young people in this hyper-rationalistic technologized world have been deprived even of the simple milestones of growing-up, since they have all the privileges and trappings of maturity from automobile to crypto-spouse by age fifteen, or, if they are of color and poor, all the pains of maturity, from rejection by the society of power to seduction by exploiting peddlers, by age fifteen. Young people are desperate for symbolic ways of leaving home that will enable everyone to accept a moment of growth as a good thing. In the absence of the creative symbols of separation and mutual acceptance, it is no wonder young and old are at war. Without the sense of ritual, without the structures of time, they do not know how to let go of each other, nor therefore how to embrace each other. In the absence of the creative symbols of separation and mutual acceptance it is no wonder the flight from the fact of death is a major industry in our culture. Ritual is the way men grapple with and come to terms with the awesome mysteries of birth, growth and death. As culture dulls our sense of ritual our sacramental heritage becomes a vestige of what once was a vibrant and passionate process of religious celebration of coming and going, of time passing.

Something similar is happening to our sense of space. Our culture at large conspires unconsciously with its highways and drive-in restaurants to make each bit of space like every other bit. Most of our buildings from the grand new Kennedy Center in Washington to the local branch of the public library have a Holiday Inn mood about them. We are losing hold of the structures of space by denying the distinctions that once told us when we were traveling and when we are home. Now we are at home everywhere and nowhere.

Ritual is a way human beings have long paid attention to the special character of specific places, to the human structures of space. Ritual happens only among people who know how to distinguish between gardens and deserts. Ritual believes in what we used to call without embarrassment "sacred space." Ritual arises from the impulse to pray spatially, which is to say, bodily. In our culture the bodily is denied; the greatest enemy of true sensuality is uniformity. We deny our bodies by making them look as much like everyone's as possible, as we deny all space by making it look like the lobby of a motel. Astroturf is capable of replacing both the garden and the desert.

Yet there is still, to use Daniel Berrigan's

phrase, a "geography of faith." There is an ecology of prayer. We must pay attention to the ways in which our very *senses* are engaged in our praying, as in all of our activity. Ritual is more than thinking. It is having a relationship to earth, other people, movement, smell, light, dark, color, the texture of stone, the sound of wind through trees. Ritual is a way of loving the places where our bodies find themselves. Ritual is a way of managing space. The uses of space in religious celebration deserve at least as much care as the uses of space in theater. The care given to the uses of space in theater is immense. The Church, who was the theater's first teacher, has lost its sense of place as it is losing its sense of time.

Respect for God and for ourselves demands the recovery of time and its moments, of space and its variations. Those of us who are looking still for Church are looking at the same time for contemplative liturgy. We are looking for ritual that goes well beyond rubric and form to the fleshing out of common memory and shared anticipation. We know that we were made to be holy, that being holy makes a person want to touch a holy time and holy space. We do not expect liturgy to form "community" or to launch political movement or to add color to a colorless life. We do expect liturgy to be holy, to be a challenge to our own lack of holiness.

Contemplative Liturgy

We can learn more than we thought we could from the old Latin Mass, though as ritual it was considerably more boring than we are likely to remember in our current fits of nostalgia. The fact is though, that, for generations down to our own, the Latin Mass was successful ritual that engaged the real structures both of time and space. The Catholic instinct for ritual has been sound, celebrating with verve and color the past, present, and future and distinctions of place—even while affirming the oneness in mystery of it all. Catholics have been good at touching the holy with care.

We have instincts that can serve us well yet in our search for significant moments of time and significant experiences of *place* for us in this universe. We *know already* how to do ritual, as we *already* begin to see the world with a kind of contemplative vision. The liturgical sensibility flies in the face of culture by celebrating the continuity between past, present and future, as it flies in the face of culture by setting aside specific places and making them different, calling them sacred. The liturgical sensibility believes in the past as it believes in the future, though our culture is embarrassed by its lack of past and is uncertain to the point of inert panic about its future.

To be honest, though, the present experience

of liturgy most of us have is something like television; you turn it on because it is there to be turned on, but nothing much happens. Because our expectations of liturgy have been raised up so high that it seems at first like a disappointment. But, when you think about it for a while the fact that "nothing much happens" at the liturgy may arise from the utter simplicity, the stripped-bare quality of the ritual that gathers us. One thing we have learned over these years of liturgical flip flops is that even when a lot of stuff "happens" not much *really* happens, and even when our "celebrations" are most spontaneous they are rigged. Having learned to expect less from the liturgy we are ready, perhaps, to discover again the center that seems to hold. The center may be where there is the least commotion but the turning there is always most rapid. The Mass in its center means three things to me: silence, story and bread. All three are precious, utterly simple, and all three are still available to us, even in the driest and most lifeless of our present worshiping communities.

Most of us find it almost impossible to be silent in this hard-driving world with our noise-polluted minds. Those of us who still "go to Mass" go in search of silence. The silence we seek is more than worldlessness or quiet; it is the world out of which the word and story spring. When a vast stillness had settled on the whole world the eternal word of God leapt down from his heavenly throne. Silence is sitting still. It is attention to the beyond in our midst. It is what used to happen to us when we entered the church, reaching for the water in the font. The silence we seek is still possible, even with the busy-ness of the new liturgy, even with the robot-like participation our new liturgists ask of us. Silence is possible when each of us declares it to himself; it can become the silence of fullness when a whole gathering of people share the declaration. People should resist the attempts of the liturgists to hide from silence. Liturgists should stop confusing silence with sullenness; people who resist our priestly cajoling for "participation" may be better artists than we are. They may prefer to sit still. The Catholic people, who by and large prefer sitting still to dancing when they worship, are yet teaching their priests something about worship. The people I serve teach me still about a kind of dancing you can do without moving. We are learning.

When real silence is dared, we can come very close to our selves and to the deep center of the world. "Nothing much happens"; what little happens comes close to everything. When it is allowed to become itself silence has a power and momentum of its own that can be startling. Vertical thinking and being replace the horizontal busy-ness of daily life. When we dare to stop talking, silence speaks. Though we are inclined to think that "nothing much happens," silence

speaks a word. It is a word that comes from
some other time and place than ours. It is a word
that comes from *real* time and *real* space; from
which, since we are not in control there, we ordinarily flee. Silence issues in a word in the way
that primordial being issues in expressive being,
in the way that God the Father issues in the Son.
When a vast stillness had settled over the whole
world, the eternal word leapt down. The mystery
repeats itself whenever we fall silent.

Christians are people who have a story about
the silence and the word. The word is for us the
story. Out of silence we speak specific words
about the Word. Our story is shocking by its
particularity; it denies all attempts to impose
religious or philosophical patterns of uniformity
on it. There is no abstraction about this flesh.
Our story is a matter of time; once on certain
days these things happened. There is a past and a
future about the story. It honors the structures of
time. Our story is a matter of space; there, at
certain places, these things happened. The story
is the way we are concrete about God, because,
as we believe, the story is the way God has been
concrete about himself.

When you look closely at the story around
which we gather, it's like looking at the gathering itself; nothing much happens. It begins with a
tribe of gypsies, tramps and thieves, one of
whom was named Jesus, who was anything but a
superstar. He lived. He died. His friends claimed

that he came back from the dead. They told stories about him. They still do. They are still gypsies, tramps and thieves, one way or the other. The great thing about the story we tell is this; in the telling we become part of it. The time and place of the story includes not only Jerusalem all those years ago, but here and now, and there and tomorrow. It includes not only Jesus and Magdalene, but ourselves. *That* is what happens when we gather for the ritual of Jesus' story. Our ritual is the recognition that the silence out of which the Word leaps is *our* silence; the Word itself is *our* word. We find ourselves gathering again and again not because so much "happens" at Mass, as if it really were a party or a picnic or a banquet, and we know it is none of those, but because the Mass tells us who we are as we tell ourselves and each other. A story is not so much. It is not a sudden opening of the sky. It is not a miracle. It is not worth media coverage. The story we tell at Mass is like air. It is what we breathe. It is what we move through when we fly and, even, when we walk. It is what we do not have when we are dead.

There is more to the story than words. There is the silence. There is the light of tall candles. There is water. There is touching stone with one knee. There is an embrace of strangers. There is the familiar gesture of a cross worn briefly by head and belly both. There is standing up. There is sitting down. It is all part of telling the story.

But the story does its turning around bread.

When everything shifts, when structures of time and space threaten to collapse, when we find ourselves wondering why we are here again, before the mute table, restless, the bread does our brown believing for us. The bread believes. We return only and eat. We touch with teeth and the hidden body the whole story; its past beginning with hunger so wrenching the gypsies ate bird droppings and called it bread from heaven; its future in which even those who are afraid to be a brother and a sister will trade gifts of food and more; its present in which the absence of God is the chief sign of his presence, making hunger the chief form of faith. Eating the bread is an act of time. An act of space. It is the Ritual at its simplest and most elaborate. It is what holds us, even now, even with our angers, in one movement yet from a common, lovely past to a promising, difficult future. The center that holds us is the act of desperation by which we say together before that bread, "Lord." Every time we do it, more happens than we know. We do not know what it means but we know it is true. The bread makes us the tribe of gypsies, tramps and thieves. It makes us the Church. It makes us, though we do not even seem to believe anymore, the gathering of saints. Communion. The bread believes. We return only and eat.

4 **THE COUNTER CULTURE CONTEMPLATES**

IT is not that contemplation is the act of looking at the world and seeing something different. Contemplation is simply a different way of seeing. Contemplation is the act of doubting what seems obvious to everyone. Contemplation refuses to live on the surface of things. It is going down and lifting up. It is the act of seeing death where there seems only to be life; seeing life where there seems only to be death. Contemplation is seeing more than is before your eyes. Seeing differently is dangerous and difficult. Seeing

differently disturbs the universe. The pursuit of a
different vision is an activity of religion that is
going on beyond "Religion" and certainly
beyond "Church." The pursuit of a different way
to see man and world is carried on by the increasingly lonely trek of exiles we have learned
to call the "counter-culture."

We must forgive each other our hackneyed
words. Counter-culture is a tired phrase, though
not yet a sales slogan. It will be soon, no doubt. I
use it to refer to that loosely gathered and un-

gathered people who find no home in the centers of power, who raise fundamental questions about prevailing values, personal and public, and who are not waiting for some bureaucratic authorization to change their way of living. The counter-culture for me refers to more than the youth-culture and the anti-war movement, although they spawned it and set its prevailing tones. The counter-culture includes the growing number of people from all backgrounds whose way of looking at their nation, their church, their own souls have changed drastically in the past ten years. Many no longer take for granted the classic idols of competition, self-grandeur, avoidance of social problems, rugged individualism, the unlimited rights of wealth and world super-powers. People who refuse to surrender their doubt and their responsibility to even the most seductive of institutions, from the department store to the school to the Church, are everywhere, and their number is growing quietly.

Cowboys and Indians

It may help to focus the differences between what we are calling "culture" and "counter-culture" to look briefly at what I think are representative metaphors in which the conflict surfaces. The counter-culture takes much of its flavor and style from young people, and its chief metaphor is one they have adopted by instinct—the Indian. The chief metaphor of prevailing American culture has long been the cowboy. It is not an accident that young people even *look* like Indians today, with their hair, headbands, fringe leather and moccasins. It is no accident that the group that tried last May to disrupt Washington the day Washington disrupted the Constitution called itself the Mayday Tribe. And it is no accident that the cowboy is the central figure in the American myth, as scholars since Turner in the last century have suggested. It was not an accidental image Richard Nixon chose when he said that getting out of Vietnam was like a cowboy backing out of a saloon with both guns blazing.

A brief comparison of some of the characteristics of cowboys and Indians will help to clarify how it is that the counter-culture has a different way of seeing the world. These characteristics, by the way, are derived more from America's mythic oracle, whose home is Hollywood, than from scientific data. The cowboys and Indians I'm talking about are not men and women but *metaphors* of conflict.

The cowboy is a loner, a Lone Ranger, a rugged individualist in the mold of Teddy (Roughrider) Roosevelt; the Indian is a tribal person, a member of a collective. The cowboy is a hero, is self-aggrandized; the Indian aggrandizes the group. The cowboy has no roots, is always moving on, in the sunset, has no lasting relationships or commitments; the Indian takes his identity from his tribal roots, from the tradition of ancestors and the hope of offspring. The cowboy is restrained, bashful. His typical expression is "yup," as Gary Cooper was fond of saying. When he sings he is detached and rigid, strumming major chords on his guitar. The Indian is ecstatic. He yells, he gestures wildly. He prizes drumbeats. He dances. The cowboy is a sexual puritan. He never kisses the "girl." He might be asexual. The Indian is polygamous. Hollywood hints that he is sexually erratic and wild. The cowboy is aggressively violent; the cowboy prizes violent conflict. Note that the Tex Ritter of our childhoods had his latest singing success with "The Ballad of Lt. Calley." The Indian is defensively violent. He stands and fights with courage, and brutality, but he does not seek the war. The cowboy has power, a gun. The Indian has less power, the bow and arrow. The cowboy is technological; he rides on a saddle. The Indian is natural; he rides bareback. The cowboy, who nearly made the buffalo extinct, exploits nature. The Indian is a partner of nature. He lives as though spirits and demons live with him in the world.

There is significance we do not see in the fact that our childhood fantasies were directed into the mythical warfare between cowboy and Indian. We can see signs of the conflict *now* between old culture adherents and new ones. What the Indians, who never had names, and the cowboys, whose names were Wild Bill, Kit, Tex and Duke, never seemed to see was that as soon as one side had to lose so the other could survive, both had already lost. Cowboys and Indians fight because they do not know mutuality is essential for human survival. As we know, cowboys murdered Indians, and, as we are beginning to realize, something in their own souls. The destiny of no young man will ever be achieved by the murder of an old. The yearnings for community, engagement and dependence which are common to us all, though we will not all admit it, will be fulfilled for one of us only when they are fulfilled for us all. As Dustin Hoffman's film "Little Big Man" suggests, cowboys and Indians may have to trade places with each other once in a while if anyone's going to make it. Or, as John Lennon says, "Don't you know it's just a fool who plays it cool when it's getting colder?"

The counter-culture is not playing it cool, even now with so much inert good order in the air. People *are* looking at their worlds differently. They are developing structures that will support their vision. The way of seeing which I have been calling "contemplative" is the way Indians see. The world with its earth, air, fire and water is alive with forces, powers and persons that no catalogue lists. People today are rediscovering what it is to touch life where there was none before.

Awe, wonder, silence and sitting still are all part of a new habit that grows. Something decisive has changed in our hearts. The world is not what we thought it was; it is neither worse, nor better. It is different and it is good. We have discovered that we are *not* cowboys. We do not prize, even in our jeans, what cowboys prize. We want neither to ruin the earth, nor to be lonely. We discover Indian instincts in our hidden selves, though we also know we are not Indians. Only Indians are Indians; they are not metaphors, but men. We learn from them, though, and discover in ourselves a pride in being alive and a love in being silent, in communion with ancestors, offspring and what we delight to call with them "spirit." The "spirit" is returning to us, and we return to the spirit.

Jesus and Drugs

For some of us this process of rediscovering a spirit-way of looking at ourselves, the world and each other has consciously *religious* dimensions. We use religious language to account for what is happening to us. We are at home with the idea that "God," our only word for our lack of words, lives here with us. It is he who demands that we see the world differently. But not all of us who are "religious" are the same. Even within the counter-culture there are ways of talking about God that have little in common with each other.

Young people who have come to be called
Jesus freaks are among those who have thrown
themselves into the new kind of religiosity that is
as remarkable for its force as for its style. You
know all about that, since Jesus has made the
cover of *Time* magazine not once but twice in the
last six months. I'm sure he is pleased. Jesus is so
fashionable that even those of us in campus ministry are preaching about him again.

If we look at the Jesus movement from the
view of the fundamentalist religion we inherit as
Americans, whether Catholic or Protestant, we
will likely be delighted by it. It accepts uncrit-
ically our strong tradition of anti-intellec-
tualism, of rigid dogmatism, of individualistic
ethics, of sexual puritanism. Like Bill Bright and
his Campus Crusade or Billy Graham and his
youth rallies or Peter Max and his Jesus Bou-
tiques or the producers of *Superstar* on Broad-
way, we will move quickly to exploit young people as American buyers and sellers are always
doing. We will do it with banners, groovy Masses
and Jesus-retreats. Young people will not be
fooled, of course, for the religion of Jesus freaks
is neither as naive nor as simple as we think it is.

If we look at the Jesus-movement from the
perspective of the despair that comes when
Americans seek community or real engagement
with social problems or mature mutuality, we
will realize that the Jesus-myth, however trivi-
alized or twisted, is a much less dangerous way

of handling loneliness, inertia and terror than is heroin. It is a tribute to the health of many young people that they have been frightened by their experiences with drugs and are using the moral absolution of a fundamentalistic Jesus to stay away from them. Drugs are the chief weapon in America's war against her own children as they have long been in the war against black people. The liberals who praise pot-smoking without dealing with the dangerous world it opens to a teenager, the parents who depend on tranquilizers, the football trainers who dispense pep pills before the game, the fakes who sell hedonistic "mysticism," the musicians who make "getting high," however you do it, a new God—they are all perpetrators of the great and dangerous lie of our time: drugs are harmless and good, only sick people misuse them. Religion, even a fundamentalist and rigid dogmatism, is preferable.

The exhilarating, ecstatic vision of Jesus that the counter-culture religious movement nourishes, partly out of its drug-flashes, is typified by wide-eyed friendliness, and unselfconscious gentleness. Jesus freaks are neither as discreet nor as embarrassed about their religious beliefs as I am. But however charming or reassuring we find the simplicity and passion of the Jesus people in their "conversion" or in their experience of "being saved," in the end their simple faith must sadden us. An inevitable disillusionment accompanies any absolutistic, authoritarian, doubt-denying world-view. What Jesus freaks who forbid any questioning or any uncertainty do now know is what we Catholics have learned at such a price over these last few years. If your moral concern does not extend beyond personal behavior to the needs of others, it is, by Jesus' own standards, immoral. If you sacrifice your *doubt* you sacrifice not only your freedom but your *self*.

Religion and Resistance

Some of us who have religious understandings of ourselves and our alienation from what we used to call the "worldly" culture are not "Jesus people," much less freaks. We *are* Christians. We are less inclined to talk about "being into God," more likely to talk about God being into us. It is a matter of whose action is primary; I'm not "into God" at all. I do hope he is "into me." We are very wary of another religious flight from social responsibility, and so we are overanxious about the political dimensions of our prayer. We prize contemplation, meditation, silence, solitude, but we trust none of it fully yet. We do not want to forget about the war, about the 300 who *still* die daily from American fire. We do not want to lose ourselves in a new hedonism of mystical pleasures. We do not want to wake up some day to our own spiritual capitalism, having hoarded the spirit and counted its blessings to death. We know from our own small experience and from our teachers, St. John, Gandhi, St. Teresa, the Jesuits and our friends in jail, that prayer and political thinking and acting go together. Contemplation and resistance. We have chosen to be faithful to both.

Active resistance to illegitimate authority, from the great movement for black equality with Dr. King to the remnant anti-war movement that even now refuses to surrender responsibility, has roots in quiet lives of prayer. Holiness is not nearly so harmless as our superiors thought it was. Holiness is what happens when the ease with which we identify ourselves with all the IBM-card categories disappears. American, male, middle class, Catholic, educated, white; I am all of the above and none. Having learned to sit still I am learning to sit loose with all our simple categories. Praying unsettles things that way.

Religion is what happens when a person dares to confront head on a point of crisis that changes the categories of creatures and the way we relate to them. Religion is what happens when everything—from the trivial, say television, to the very heavy, say the war—comes under the judgment of God. The counter-culture has been a point of crisis like that for many people. It has been for me. I am not the person I thought I was. It is not that we have replaced "culture" with its "counter" or one set of punch cards with another. We have learned again that only God is God. It is his hard judgment we seek, but that begins with our own. In this *process* even the idols of the idol smashers get smashed. I loved the idol-smashers until they smashed me. Now I fear what we can do to ourselves in the name of God. If you want to hit me do it in your own name, not his. God is no bureaucracy. But I'd rather be self-righteous than apathetic, I'd rather be a hammer than a nail. But really, I'd rather not be either. Religion is what happens when we refuse to be.

The point of crisis in which I have begun to be myself has come to me in the flesh of various men and women who have taught me the old lesson that prayer is wrestling with God. Lots of people like me have found their points of change and religious movement in the contemplatives who find themselves in prison or in other forms of high jeopardy now. It is wrong for us to make heroes of them, for that is a way of hiding behind them. Yet neither our lives nor our hopes would be the same if names like Berrigan, King, Chavez, Mullaney, Walsh, Coffin, Parilla, Helder Camara and Torres were unknown to us. We believe still in the power of the spirit to move through the Church in part because the spirit moves through them. It is the same spirit we detect now and then at motion in ourselves. We are frightened of it partly, but also welcoming, for it is the spirit whose uncertain wrestling teaches us humanity. Discovering the limits of our own deep center, the spirit calls us to its edge in the name of, not "God" or the "poor," but our own best selves. We are the *Church*, proud to be and humble, glad to be and frightened. Whatever forms of jeopardy or risk that meeting of flesh and spirit leads to, whether large or small, we are not the same again. Nor is anything. We have begun *to see* differently. We have begun an act of contemplation which is our first act of resistance.

Some say that the religious people who still refuse to be quiet about the war and who go around with their self-righteous carping are just the same old absolutistic, puritanical, judgmental Catholics of the old days. Perhaps. It is true that I think of myself and some friends as "Pilgrims of the Absolute," to use Leon Bloy's phrase. I do not possess the absolute, but I do seek it, even as I fear its judgment.

There are rigorous instincts and absolute demands to which men and women *must* respond. We have a conviction that the worst enemy of man is not self-righteousness but inertia. Bloy wrote, "I am not qualified to judge people, you say; am I to infer from this cheap sophism that I am not even qualified to see and that it is forbidden me to raise an arm against an incendiary who, filled with confidence in my brotherly inertia, is about to set off before my eyes a mine that will destroy an entire city?" Perhaps when a man stands up when everything tries to keep him lying down, an edge of self-righteousness is part of the price he pays. "Hypocrisy," according to Duc de la Rochefoucauld, "is the tribute vice pays to virtue." If we have no ideals, no commitments, no passions, no dreams, no fierce loves, we will definitely not be hypocrites. We will definitely not be self-righteous. Nor will we be religious.

What is important about the commitment of religious people to resist the acts of illegitimate authority wherever they occur is that they have both a tradition and a vision that can support the lifetime effort to enshrine an alternate way of looking at man in alternate social structures. The great service that the Church-reborning can do this weary world is to offer a concrete source of identity and support to people who do not want simply to slip into their assigned place in the vast bureaucracy. I do not know whether my ecclesiology is respectable. I do know that the Church is still of great service *to me*, for it tells me, even as I wonder, who I am. The Church enables me to touch the silence, the Story, the Bread, and the doubt, all of which call into question the structures of my own personal life and the structures of society, even as they shake with the stresses of our time.

This Church-reborning is "The Church Against Itself," to use Rosemary Radford

Ruether's phrase. The check against its own hypocrisy is the fact that the Church is always judged by its own words, by the word it serves. It lives with the sense of its own lack of faithfulness to its own call. The Church is always judged by its own center, which is the memory of Jesus Christ and his present Spirit. Always judged and always found wanting. Always in pilgrimage toward the absolute, never in possession of it. The Church reborning is not only counter-culture, but counter-church.

In judgment, in truth, especially when it is the gospel judgment called love, we discover not only our continuing lack of nerve but the rather surprising survival of our strength. The Church, by God, even as its habits and common flesh are peeled off in the dying of its sub-worlds, is still the Church. The gospel of Jesus Christ is still proclaimed. The vision of silence and solitude which sets restless souls to peace and peaceful ones to restlessness is still shared. Acts of self-sacrifice and courage and great daring are still happening in the name of men and God. People still pray. We are still worshipers.

To accept and to continue to accept the call to ministry within the Church is to believe that the ghost of the Church is mixed in with the Spirit of God. Ministry is an act of hope that the ghost can be set free. The Church can be itself. Ministry also believes that the movement for a changed world, implying both the hard destruction of old habits and institutions as well as the long haul nurturing of new ones, that that movement of liberation enshrines for us the holiness of spirit-life. Yet it needs, I dare to say it, Churching, for Churching is the risk by which we name our centers with the name of God. The call to be fully human is a call to stand in faith before God naming him. Ministry may not know what that means, but only that it is necessary. Prayerfulness and shrewd politics. If our revolution is to be humane it must be holy.

We are called to be contemplative and to be counter-culture. When they are real they are moments of the same movement. They are the ways in which we pay attention to that deep breath breathing in us now, contemplating, countering. The promise of spirit to which we cling means that there will always be a counter-church, always be contemplation. Always begins now. There are good signs that point yet to the faithful presence of spirit in our midst.

One of the best is that young men and women who once would have entered seminaries and convents no longer do, but instead pursue full life and religious dedication in new ways. I know many young men and women like that myself, and so, I suspect, do you. The most serious task facing those of us who still believe in the Church-reborning is to *enable* and support the call God *still* gives men and women to serve him. Ministry has come full circle to mean developing new structures for ministry in which men *and* women can sustain the contemplative vision *and* the resisting impulse God still plants in their souled flesh. The bishops will not do it until the Church does. There are new ways of being religious which are not pious. There are new ways of being called which may not be "vocation." There are new ways of being Catholic which are not "Churchy."

I rejoice to be here. It is that old transfiguring impulse. God is at it again. Look at you! You are alive! Indeed you are a kind of glory! Look at me! Laughing yet! This is no mountain top, we know that for sure. It is no time for pitching tents or settling down. It is time, at once, for silence, song, sitting still and moving on. The world and our way of being in it are good. For now that is all we know or need to know of God.